RESOURCING

Handbook for
Special Education
Resource Teachers

Mary Yeomans Jackson

Published by
The Council for Exceptional Children

Library of Congress Cataloging-in-Publication Data

Jackson, Mary Yeomans.
  Resourcing : handbook for special education resource teachers /
Mary Yeomans Jackson.
    p. cm.
  ISBN 0-86586-219-2
  1. Special education teachers—United States—Handbooks, manuals,
etc. 2. Teaching—Aids and devices—Handbooks, manuals, etc.
3. Special education—United States. I. Title.
LC3969.J33   1992
371.9—dc20   91-44861

Stock No. P366

Printed in the United States of America

10   9   8   7   6   5   4   3   2

About the Author

Mary Yeomans Jackson is a Director of Special Programs in the Fort Bend Independent School District, Sugar Land, Texas. She has been a resource room teacher, diagnostician, supervisor, consultant, director of West Central Center, Georgia Learning Resources System, and a special education mediator. She has worked with resource teachers in numerous schools in Georgia, Texas, and the Department of Defense Dependents' schools. Ms. Jackson received her master's degree in special education from Georgia State University in Atlanta.

Other contributors are the outstanding educators—her dear friends and cohorts—who have, over the years, been her source of creativity, support, solace, and laughter. In particular, her thanks go to the late Marjorie Westbrook, Sargent, Georgia; to Betsy Primm, Director of Metro East GLRS, Atlanta, Georgia and her secretarial staff for their assistance in this project, and to Dillee Duncan for her outstanding secretarial skills.

Dedication

This book is dedicated to all

"resource teachers"
"resource room teachers"
"special education resource teachers"
"interrelated teachers"
"etc."

I know—your titles change;

your place—the resource room—often changes;
your students change;
your identity changes;
your position within the school has changed;
your job is difficult!

Hopefully, this book can be a resource to you in suggesting ways to

be a resource to yourself;
be a resource to others; and
be a user of resources.

Contents

Introduction

WHY A BOOKLET ON RESOURCING?

Evidence suggests that the teacher in the resource room is often stressed! This should not come as a surprise, given the fact that special education has come

OUT OF THE CLOSETS . . .

Special education teachers have moved from isolated backrooms, basements, and broom closets where they spent all day with a group of students with special educational needs. In the past, there was not much interaction, if any, with the rest of the school. The job was to work with the students and keep them "out of the way." Special education teachers *belonged* to their students in their room.

Through the years, special education teachers have moved up and out into the school world. They *and* their students flow in and out of the hallways, lunchrooms, and classrooms and interact with the rest of the school. Special education classes are no longer isolated and cannot be ignored. Special education teachers no longer belong just to their students, they are in the mainstream of schools.

AND INTO THE MAINSTREAM . . .

Now that special education has "arrived," the job of the special education teacher has changed. The special education teacher is not just a teacher of children with special needs in a special education room shut off from the rest of the school.

Many of you are now in what is called a *resource room setting.* Your students flow into and out of your room as well as mainstream into regular education classes. You have to interact with regular education personnel. Your job entails not only teaching these students in your classroom but also keeping up with them throughout the day, wherever they may be. You are not in the school just to teach these students. You are the special education expert in the school—the *resource teacher.*

Webster's dictionary defines "resource" as "a new or a reserve source of supply or support; a possibility of relief or recovery; an ability to meet and handle a situation; something to which one has recourse in difficulty."

And therein lies a problem: reducing the stress.

Being called a "resource teacher" sets up expectations for yourself and for others regarding who you are. You have essentially been defined as a resource and so has your room. The expectation is that you are the resource, and the relief, to special education students, teachers in the school, parents, other school personnel, agency personnel, and yourself. Your identity is scattered. You are "teacher," "collaborator," "resource room manager," "team member," and many other people.

You consider yourself a resource teacher, yet how do you do it all? How can you teach your students and still be an effective resource within the school? In order to be an effective teacher, you know it is necessary for you to be a resource to others outside your classroom. Yet this is difficult. You are pulled in many directions, and the demands placed upon you are extensive. Can you do it all, do it well, and do it without all the stress? This book about resourcing is designed to help you.

On the following pages are some suggestions to assist you in your resourcing. You have the teaching experience. You have had the training for teaching students in special education. You know your responsibilities within the class-room. These things will not be addressed. What *is* addressed is your job as a resource within the school at large. "Resourcing," according to the author, means

"taking in"
"extending out"
"being resourceful"
"being a source" . . .

for yourself, your students, school staff, parents, and other related persons.

1

Being a Resource to Yourself

In order to be a resource to others, you must first be a resource to yourself. Your strength and effectiveness as a resource teacher hinge upon your being confident and secure in your role as a resource. If you are a new teacher, you are probably feeling somewhat insecure in your new job. This is to be expected. Do not panic! Your confidence will grow daily as you successfully meet the needs of your students and gain the trust and respect of your colleagues. If you are an experienced teacher, you may also feel some insecurity as your role shifts to being a resource within the school. Whether you are a new or experienced teacher, your confidence also will grow as you explore your feelings about this new role and as you make decisions about how you will implement your resourcing goals.

HOW DO YOU FEEL ABOUT THIS ROLE?

There are a number of questions you need to ask yourself—and answer—if you choose to be a resource to others as well as to yourself. By answering these questions you will know where you stand and what being a resource means to you.

If you see a need to be a resource in your job setting and think that it is important, then you are well on your way to establishing ways to be a resource to yourself and others. Being a resource comes from a conviction and confidence that this is an important role for you. You need to see it as helpful and necessary in assisting students with special needs.

A positive attitude is a must—for your own sanity and that of others. If you do not see your resourcing role as important and do not have a positive attitude toward this role, then it will be a burden every time you are called on to provide resources. Personnel and parents may sense that it is a burden for you; they may feel shortchanged and may regret that they contacted you. This can affect their relationship with your students. As a result, you might experience the following symptoms:

Increased stress	Anger
Tiredness	Headaches
Frustration	Feelings of inadequacy

The importance of clarifying your role as a resource—your goals and objectives—cannot be overstated. If you know who you are as a professional and where you are going, your job will be easier and your effectiveness will increase in the following ways:

- You will be operating from a position of strength; that is, you will know who you are as a professional and what you want.

- Your goals will be clearly defined and thus your rewards and accomplishments will be easy to spot.

- You will save time—time you may have spent in the past trying to figure out just who you are in your school.

- Your students, your colleagues, and your students' parents will sense your confidence and self-assurance and trust will be facilitated.

- In essence, *you* will be a resource to yourself.

HOW DO YOU ACHIEVE THIS SENSE OF CONFIDENCE REGARDING YOUR RESOURCING ROLE?

As mentioned earlier, there are some questions you need to consider in terms of being a resource. The questionnaire that begins on page 3 is designed to assist you in this endeavor. Its purpose is to

- Assist you in exploring your feelings about the issue of resourcing.

- Help you establish a clear picture of yourself in this role.

- Give you an opportunity to analyze yourself in terms of your strengths, weaknesses, beliefs, and other issues.

- Help you structure your "plan" in carrying out this role.

- Reinforce your conviction that you can be effective in this role.

Following the questionnaire, there is a discussion of each item to assist you in exploring the various issues surrounding your role as a resource. You may decide to complete the questionnaire first and then read the discussion, or you may answer each question as you read the corresponding section dealing with that item. Again, the discussion of each question is included to assist you as you explore your own feelings and convictions about resourcing. This is an opportunity for you to reach your own conclusions about how you are going to fulfill your role as a resource teacher and to make decisions about the who's, what's, when's and where's of your job and how to accomplish your professional goals.

Keep in mind that this self-analysis is designed to help you untangle the frustrating, multipurpose job you now have and to help you put your many roles and functions in perspective. It can help you "take good care of yourself" while being an effective, self-assured professional. It is a start to being a resource to yourself.

YOUR PERSONAL RESOURCING QUESTIONNAIRE

1. Do I see resourcing as important in my job?

   ____ Yes   ____ No

   If "yes," continue to item 2.

   If "no," list below your reasons why:

   If "no," what effect will my decision not to be a resource have on my students, the school, and me?

2. Why is it important that I be a resource? What will be the rewards to me, to my students, to other personnel if I choose this role for myself?

3. What does being a resource mean to me?

   A. How can I fulfill my role as a resource within the school? (Check the items that apply.)

      ____ Provide information on my program and students to school personnel, parents, and others.

      ____ Serve as a "resource center" providing ideas, techniques, and materials to assist mainstream students.

      ____ Provide direction services (information on agencies, programs, etc.) to assist students with disabilities.

      ____ Participate actively on Child Study Teams, Teacher Assistance Teams, and others.

      ____ "Sell" my program.

      ____ Be a support, a "friendly ear," to regular educators.

      ____ Work with agency personnel and parents in assisting learners with disabilities.

Note: From *Resourcing: Handbook for Special Education Resource Teachers* by Mary Yeomans Jackson, 1992, Reston, VA: The Council for Exceptional Children. Reprinted by permission.

     ____ Assist my students with regular education assignments.

     ____ Other (please specify). _____

B. To whom can I be a resource? (Check those that apply.)

     ____ Regular education teachers

     ____ Support personnel (psychologists, counselors, social workers, etc.)

     ____ My students

     ____ Administrators (principals, special education directors, curriculum directors, etc.)

     ____ Other (please specify). _____

4. What are my strengths in terms of being a resource within the school? (Check those that apply.)

     ____ Good communication skills

     ____ Status as accepted, respected member of the school staff

     ____ Knowledge and possession of lots of resources for staff, parents, other personnel

     ____ Creativity

     ____ High energy level

     ____ Good organizational skills

     ____ Good interpersonal skills

     ____ Ability to function as an effective team member

     ____ Willingness, eagerness to share ideas and resources

     ____ Knowledge of mainstreaming techniques

     ____ Other (please specify). _____

5. What are my weaknesses in terms of being a resource within the school? (Check those that apply.)

     ____ Lack of knowledge and skills in providing resources

Note: From *Resourcing: Handbook for Special Education Resource Teachers* by Mary Yeomans Jackson, 1992, Reston, VA: The Council for Exceptional Children. Reprinted by permission.

_____ Lack of materials and resources to assist others in working with people who have disabilities

_____ Tendency to isolate myself within the school

_____ Difficulty in working with peers

_____ Lack of knowledge regarding the regular education curriculum, expectations for students, and similar issues

_____ Poor organizational skills

_____ Burnout

_____ A need to do it all myself and to do it my way

_____ Other (please specify). _____

6. How receptive is the school climate to my providing resources?

7. What are my greatest fears regarding the fulfillment of my role as a resource within the school?

8. What factors work against me in fulfilling this role? (Check those that are most problematic.)

_____ Myself (see 5, 7 above)

_____ The school climate (see 6)

_____ Turf-guarding

_____ Time

_____ Lack of funds

_____ Lack of support

_____ Number of demands placed upon me already

_____ Absence of need for resources on school's part

_____ Other (please specify). _____
_____

Note: From _Resourcing: Handbook for Special Education Resource Teachers_ by Mary Yeomans Jackson, 1992, Reston, VA: The Council for Exceptional Children. Reprinted by permission.

9. What factors do I have working for me?

_____ Myself (4)

_____ The school climate (6)

_____ A high need for resources within the school

_____ Support

_____ A well-organized class

_____ Other (please specify). _____

_____

10. How can I overcome the obstacles I have identified? (questions 5, 7, 8)

11. Given my answers to the previous questions (taking into consideration my attitude toward this role, my strengths and weaknesses, the school climate, obstacles in the way, factors that support me, etc.), what goals do I have for myself in being a resource? What are my objectives? My priorities?

Objectives:

Priorities:

12. Finally, given my goals, how much am I responsible for as a resource and how much of the responsibility lies elsewhere?

Note: From *Resourcing: Handbook for Special Education Resource Teachers* by Mary Yeomans Jackson, 1992, Reston, VA: The Council for Exceptional Children. Reprinted by permission.

FURTHER THOUGHTS ON RESOURCING

1. Do I See Resourcing as Important?

This question is basic. You probably work with each of your students from 45 minutes to an hour each day. That leaves a lot of time when they are not with you. Could you be helpful to them when they are not in your class? In particular, is there a need for you to work with regular educators who have your students in their classes? We all know that regular educators have a tough job. They are faced with students who have varying abilities and attitudinal, behavioral, and motivational characteristics. Often, regular educators have not been trained to deal with students who have special needs, such as those who are slow to learn, those who are mainstreamed, those with behavioral problems, or those who are unmotivated. Do you have resources and skills that could be helpful to these teachers and, as a result, to your students? Are there other staff members who could benefit from your resources? Could being a resource help *you*? Perhaps, you would feel a greater sense of belonging in the school if you moved into the mainstream. Positive results from your resourcing might also increase your feelings of accomplishment. The benefits to your students, in particular, might ease the frustration you feel when they do not experience success in the mainstream.

Finally, do you have an obligation to be a resource given federal and state regulations, the least restrictive environment mandate, and research findings on mainstreaming that show the positive benefits for students when regular and special educators work collaboratively?

Your answer to question 1 depends, at least somewhat, on your feelings regarding these issues. Your particular job situation may or may not require you to be a resource outside your classroom; however, it is an issue that you should clarify for yourself. To be an effective resource, you need to feel that the role is important for you in your job. If you do not feel it is important, you need to think about how this attitude impacts on you and your students. I would suggest that you spend some time talking with other resource teachers who *do* see the importance of an expanded role for themselves outside the classroom. Read the literature on collaboration, inclusion, and mainstreaming. Evaluate yourself in terms of your fears and concerns regarding this role. If you still do not feel it is important, then make sure you *know* you can be effective with your students during the time you have them in your classroom.

2. Why Is It Important That I Be a Resource? What Will Be the Rewards to Me, to My Students, to Other Personnel If I Choose This Role for Myself?

If you have answered "yes" to question 1, you must have some reasons in mind as to why it is important to you and others. Putting these into writing can give you a clearer picture of your personal goals in this role. You will also be better able to gauge your effectiveness as a resource in that you can spot rewards and benefits when they occur. The clarification of such benefits will strengthen your convictions regarding the importance of your role as resource and add to the sureness from which you operate. The following are some possible benefits to consider:

For yourself:

- Becoming a valuable, worthwhile part of the staff.
- Diversification of your job responsibilities.
- Increased self-esteem from assisting others.
- Feelings of accomplishment.
- Increased interpersonal contact with peers.
- Increased knowledge.
- Positive benefits that come from sharing.
- Increased positive feedback from other persons including students, faculty, support personnel, and parents.

For your students:

- More success in the mainstream.
- Feelings of being supported throughout the day.
- Less frustration.
- Clearer understanding of their responsibilities in the regular education environment.

For other personnel:

- Increased knowledge and skills in meeting the needs of students with disabilities.
- Increased feelings of support from special education personnel.
- Clearer delineation of their roles and responsibilities and yours regarding students with disabilities.
- Feelings of self-esteem in working with you to plan for students.
- Feelings that they have something worthwhile to share.
- Less frustration in working with students with disabilities.

3. What Does "Being a Resource" Mean to Me?

If you think being a resource is important . . . and if you think this role will result in benefits to you and others, then . . . you probably have a pretty good idea of what it means to be a resource. However, it should be helpful to you to further clarify *exactly* what being a resource means in terms of your fulfilling this new role now and in the future.

Question 3A addresses the function of this role. When answering this question, you should brainstorm the various ways in which you might be a resource. At this point, you should identify a range of possibilities that you may or may not choose to carry out in your job. Think of resources that could be made available that you have not thought about before. You might also want to compare your answers with those of other colleagues.

Possible resources that you might provide include the following:

- Student-use materials.
- Professional materials.
- Consultative services.
- Informational materials.
- Support services.
- Participation and/or leadership in teacher support teams.
- Direction to other resources and services.
- Instructional services.
- (Add your own.)

Question 3B addresses the issue of persons to whom resources might be provided. Your target group may vary depending on the type of resources needed and your own goals. An obvious target group is regular educators, especially those currently working with students who have been mainstreamed. If you are just beginning your role as a resource, you may want to delineate this group further, however. You do not want to set yourself up to fail, and by approaching the school's entire faculty you may be taking on too much. The general suggestion is to consider first those teachers you feel will be most receptive to your efforts, get their support, and then branch out. You may only have one teacher in mind; that is acceptable too. You have a "feel" for your school staff, and you should pay attention to it.

Support personnel could also benefit from your resources. You certainly are already working with psychologists, counselors, or social workers, but perhaps there are other ways in which you and these professionals can work together to meet the needs of students with disabilities. You probably have already given them some information on your students, but are there other resources that could be helpful to them—resources of which they may not be aware?

Other support persons in the school include the janitor, food service staff, secretarial staff, or bus drivers. Although your resources will not necessarily be targeted to this group, their cooperation and support is invaluable. Not only can they help you amass resources, they can also facilitate some objectives for your students. For example, behavioral programs may be implemented in the cafeteria, and the staff there can help you in observing the students and perhaps giving reinforcers. In return, you might provide them with training, special attention, and support. You might also provide them with a student helper who can be learning social and work skills while providing a service.

Administrators often have hectic jobs and are required to fulfill numerous responsibilities. Are there ways in which you could help them lighten their load? Could "selling" your program to them improve the school environment for your students? Could the resources you have available be directed through administrators to assist a wider audience?

Parents often call on you, and you meet with them regularly. Could these contacts be more structured to ensure positive benefits to your students? Are there ways to increase parent participation?

Personnel from other agencies might also benefit from your resources. Many times they are in need of information on resources available and also need a contact person in the schools. Your students may be involved with other agencies. Cooperative relations with these agencies could prove beneficial for the students. How could you help such agency personnel?

4. What Are My Strengths in Terms of Being a Resource Within a School?

If you look back at your answers to questions 1 through 3, you have an idea about what being a resource entails for you. In thinking about the possible ways you could fulfill this role, you can see that certain skills, knowledge, and characteristics will be required on your part. You have a lot going for you. Take this time and identify your strengths. In doing so, you will see that:

- You already have a lot of what it takes to be an effective resource.

- You will *know* what your strengths are and you can accentuate them to your advantage in meeting your goal.

- You can identify some possible areas where you need to improve.

- You can be more confident that you *can* be a resource.

To be a resource, you have to work with other people. Look at your interpersonal skills: Are you a good communicator? Do you work well with people? Do you have a knack for putting people at ease? Are you a good listener? Look at your current status within the school. To be a resource, you do not have to be the most powerful or the most respected. In fact, too much power can be intimidating. However, you do need to have inroads with the staff and be accepted at least to some extent. If a sociogram were done of your staff, where would you stand? What resources do you already have that you could share? These include human resources (your knowledge, skills, and support) as well as physical resources (books and handouts).

Also look at yourself in terms of your energy, creativity, and organizational skills. You need to assess your current position in terms of how prepared you are to move out into the mainstream. You have probably got your own classes going well, and your teaching is effective. These are strengths. By "having your own house in order," you are in an excellent position to expand your role as resource teacher. You have had experience in scheduling, writing goals, and creatively developing programs. These are assets in terms of resourcing. Give yourself credit for these strengths!

5. What Are My Weaknesses?

This is not an exercise designed to discourage you. Keep your strengths in mind and objectively consider possible weaknesses that could get in the way of your being an effective resource. It is important that you know which of your characteristics can sabotage your efforts and sidetrack you. By knowing these, you can prevent a lot of stress and frustration. If you identify your weaknesses, you can:

- Work on correcting them.
- Learn ways to work around them.
- Be more forgiving of yourself.
- Objectively assess what you can and cannot do.

One weakness you might have identified is a lack of knowledge and skills in providing resources. Many of us have not been trained to be resources, so this could well be an area of need. Fortunately, there are lots of ways to obtain this information and it will be discussed later in this book.

Isolation is often something teachers inadvertently fall into. Resource rooms are sometimes placed in out-of-the-way areas of school buildings. In such circumstances, it is easy to retreat into the classroom and forget the outside world. If the staff has a negative attitude toward special education, this isolation becomes self-protective and understandable. A teacher's own fears and insecurities can also perpetuate this enclosed attitude.

Interpersonal skills may also be an area in which you could make improvements. It is safe to say that not everyone is a Leo Buscaglia or Carl Rogers. If you are a teacher, you obviously have some good interpersonal skills. However, some areas may be difficult for you. For example, you may find it difficult to make contacts assertively with colleagues. Their abrupt manner or lack of interest may overwhelm you in your efforts to be a resource. On the other hand, you may like to be in control and have a tendency to take charge. Sometimes, turf-guarding and specialized knowledge gets in the way of working *with* colleagues.

Perhaps you are already burned out or tired. Have you given up? Teaching special education students is tiring: It takes a *lot* to be an effective teacher. Your efforts to work with others in your school may have been thwarted in the past. Does just thinking about moving out into the mainstream make you utter a huge sigh?

Look at your weaknesses objectively and *make sure you keep in mind your strengths!*

6. How Receptive Is the School Climate to My Providing Resources?

Some schools flow with a sense of camaraderie, good cheer, and an air of faculty support and interaction. This kind of atmosphere fosters the sharing of skills and ideas among teachers. It is an ideal situation for a resource teacher who wants to move out into the mainstream.

On the other end of the continuum is the school that is very closed. Teachers have their classes and their rooms and are expected to "take care of their own." The faculty may be somewhat interactive, but not in the sense of having a cooperative working relationship. Such an atmosphere makes it difficult to share resources because everyone is responsible for his or her own territory.

Of course, schools vary as to their openness and receptivity to cooperative planning and sharing. Often it is the administrator in the school who sets the tone. In looking at your own school's climate, try to determine where your principal stands in terms of fostering cooperation and shared activities among the staff. Would this person support your efforts and assist you? Is the attitude of the school staff open or closed in terms of receptivity to cooperative activities? Do students have to fit the curriculum or vice versa? Does the prevailing attitude encourage adaptations for students with special problems or imply that these students belong elsewhere? How often are you approached for resources and ideas to assist students? How have your efforts to share been regarded? Is there a core of teachers who would be willing to work with you?

Depending on your answers to these questions, your goals as a resource may vary. If your school has a closed atmosphere, you have your work cut out for you. But success is not impossible! You will just have to begin at a different place than your fortunate cohorts who work in a more open climate.

7. What Are My Greatest Fears Regarding the Fulfillment of My Role as a Resource Within the School?

When taking on new roles, teachers are sometimes fearful of the changes that will be required. Although the challenge of taking on new responsibilities is often energizing and rewarding, it can also threaten the status quo and the confidence you feel in your present position. When taking on any new role, it is helpful to clarify and deal with any fears you may have. This will diminish the fears and allow you to take steps to avoid the possibility that the fears will be realized.

When you think of yourself moving into your new role as resource, you may have some fears regarding your success. These might include the following:

- Rejection by the staff (i.e., they do not need your help).
- Lack of skills to accomplish the task.
- Detrimental effects on your own teaching program (i.e., it will take time you should be spending on planning for your own classroom activities).
- The possibility that too much will be asked of you.

No matter what your fears may be (and you may not have any), address them objectively and realistically. Recognizing legitimate concerns about a new job role can be helpful to you. You are in a better position to ensure your success if you have addressed potential pitfalls and problem areas. Fears do not have to be debilitating, and they can be instigators for better planning and preparation prior to assuming new roles. Use them to your advantage and you will be ahead of the game!

8. What Factors Work Against Me in Fulfilling This Role?

The last few questions you have answered have dealt with possible negative aspects of assuming the role of a resource. Hopefully, you have not lost heart and decided to give up on this endeavor. One theory is that people often jump into projects before considering all the factors involved. As a result, they are sidetracked or demoralized by factors that interfere with progress—factors that could have been recognized, prior to beginning a new endeavor. Your preplanning and recognition of where you are will help you avoid potential disasters and increase your chances for success.

What might sidetrack you or get in the way of your successful implementation of this role? Is it yourself? The school situation? A lack of the ways and means to fulfill this role? You may want to lay this all out before you objectively and fairly. Having done so, you can plan corrective action.

9. What Factors Do I Have Working for Me?

You have considered the negatives involved in assuming the role of resource. These negatives will not overcome your resolve if you also consider the positives. A healthy, balanced consideration of strengths and weaknesses puts things into perspective and helps you form a plan of action that will lead to success.

What factors work *for* you? You know you have strengths that will help you succeed. Go back to question 4 and look at your positives. Also think of other positives in your school. Are there characteristics of your school that will work to your advantage? What resourcing needs does the school have that you could easily address with success? Name the staff members you can count on for support. Having your own house in order is also a plus. The fact that your classes run smoothly and effectively puts less pressure on you both mentally and physically.

These positives can serve you in good stead, and you can fall back on them when and if you need them. They also increase your confidence level. Your role as a resource will be easier if you make sure you have the positives in mind and accentuate them!

10. How Can I Overcome Obstacles to My Success? (see Q. 5-8.)

You have considered your pluses and minuses, and you now have in mind some problem areas that could interfere with your success as a resource. What are your major obstacles? These should be dealt with first. Do these obstacles relate to you personally? If so, how can you address and deal with them? For example, do you feel that you do not have the necessary resources and skills available to serve you well in this role? Chapter 3 will give you suggestions on accessing resources, but there are also other ways to increase your skills. Do you have peers who are already assuming the role of resource? Could they assist you? Is there a course available at a nearby college or university that would be helpful? Is anyone in your area offering workshops or inservice training on this topic? Could you visit a model project? In looking at your strengths, do you have the skills but just need to accentuate them and put them into the framework of a resourcing role?

Are there problems relative to your school situation that might get in the way of your serving in this resourcing function? Perhaps you feel a lack of support for such a role from your school's staff. Think of the staff individually. Is there one person who might be more open to your efforts? Do you need to make a presentation, "sell" your program to your principal and/or faculty? Is there one activity you could do, one resource you could share that you know would be received positively by the staff? Remember, you do not have to run a total resource program and work with every teacher in beginning this endeavor. You do not want to overwhelm yourself.

Is dealing with multiple supervisors a problem? As a resource teacher you probably have several persons overseeing your program—the principal, the special education director and coordinator, and the department head. Do you need clarification of your chain of command? Can you elicit support from all of these persons and further increase your opportunities for success? Can one of them assist you in dealing effectively with another who may not be as supportive? Clear communication channels with all of these persons will be an asset. Not only can they clear paths for you, they can also be an important source of ideas and resources.

Do you lack time? Is your day so scheduled that there are not any extra minutes in the day to assume this role? Look at your schedule. Can you rearrange your day? Is there any time before or after school hours? Could you work with another special education teacher and arrange a schedule whereby the two of you could switch off, taking each other's students once or twice a week and giving each other some free time? Is yours just a time-management problem? Could you get assistance in organizing your time more efficiently?

Try to brainstorm possibilities for overcoming your obstacles. If you cannot resolve your problem, could you take another direction in terms of your resourcing role? Could you take this one problem and make it your goal to resolve it this year? Perhaps this groundwork is necessary prior to beginning your resource program. If you are still roadblocked by obstacles, confer with colleagues. Perhaps they have suggestions. Remember, your goal as a resource is to make it a role in which you can be effective and one that serves your school's needs. Do not set yourself up to fail. Do what you can to proceed systematically and successfully.

11. What Are My Objectives and Priorities?

If you have gone through this questionnaire, answering each question in a thoughtful, honest manner, you have amassed quite a bit of information about yourself and your role as a resource. Congratulations! You are off to an excellent start because you now know where you are and have a good idea of where you are going. This is a good point at which to write down and clarify your goals and priorities. Question 11 gives you space to jot down your goals and objectives. On the following pages are some worksheets you can use to further clarify your plan.

What are your long-term goals? In the best of all possible worlds, what would you want your resource role to encompass? What would you want to accomplish? Look back at your answer to question 3. Are the items you checked your ultimate goals? Once you have established your goals, look at where you are now. What are your priorities? Where do you want to begin? What is most important? Is there a particular area in which your energies could be focused to provide the most benefit to the greatest number of mainstreamed students? Where can you start successfully? Try to look at it from the perspective of only this school year. What could you do this year? Next year? Further down the road?

Now, take your long-term goals and develop the set of short-term objectives to achieve each one. This sounds like an individualized education program, doesn't it? Well, you have certainly had practice at writing IEPs, so why not write one for yourself? Think of the steps you must take to achieve your goal. Write them down. What is the time framework for each? When can you realistically begin to work on your goal and approximately how long will it take? It may be an ongoing goal or it may be just a preliminary activity that, once accomplished, will not be repeated. What will you need to help you accomplish this goal? Resources? The involvement of other people? Paperwork? Who will be your target audience? You may want to be quite specific here. Are there certain teachers you will begin with? Parents? Administrators? Finally, how will you know that your goal has been accomplished? How will you define "success"?

Example

Long-Term Goal:	To provide instructional resources to teachers working with mainstreamed students.
Short-Term Objective:	Establish a library of resource materials to assist regular educators.
Time Framework:	Set up library September–November. Begin lending program December 1. Continue to end of school year.
Things Needed:	Professional materials on mainstreaming. Instructional strategies. High interest/low vocabulary content area books. Handouts. Access to resource centers.
Target Audience:	Teachers working with my students in the mainstream.
Criteria for Success:	By end of year, 100% of target audience will have used library at least once; 80% of target audience will have used library at least twice monthly; 80% of target audience will find the resource library "helpful" as reported on a written evaluation.

RESOURCE ACTIVITIES

DATE: _____

PRIORITIZED LONG-TERM GOALS
(What I want to accomplish as a resource)

1. _____
2. _____
3. _____
4. _____
5. _____

LONG-TERM GOAL (NUMBER)	SHORT-TERM OBJECTIVES TO ACHIEVE THIS GOAL	TIME FRAMEWORK	WHAT I NEED TO ACCOMPLISH THIS GOAL	TARGET GROUP	HOW I WILL EVALUATE MY EFFECTIVENESS

Note: From *Resourcing: Handbook for Special Education Resource Teachers* by Mary Yeomans Jackson, 1992, Reston, VA: The Council for Exceptional Children. Reprinted by permission.

MY GOALS AS A RESOURCE

Goal:

Time Required:

Resources I Will Need:

Persons Needed to Assist Me in This Goal:

Target Audience:

Pre-Implementation Needs:

Implementation Activities:

Possible Rewards for Me/My Students:

Things I Will Need to Watch Out for:

How I Will Sell This Idea:

Ways I Can Increase My Chances for Success:

Ways I Have to Keep Myself Sane While Implementing This Activity:

Note: From *Resourcing: Handbook for Special Education Resource Teachers* by Mary Yeomans Jackson, 1992, Reston, VA: The Council for Exceptional Children. Reprinted by permission.

12. Finally, Given My Goals, How Much Am I Responsible for as a Resource?

This is an important question to consider as you establish your goal of providing resources. In the past, special education has often set itself up as the salvation for students with disabilities. Special educators have assumed responsibility for these students and essentially said to regular educators, "Give us your students with problems; we'll take care of them." With the passage of Public Law 94-142, the tables turned somewhat, and special educators went back to regular educators and said, "Our kids need your services; they have been too isolated . . . let us give them back to you for at least part of the time." This move has, in many cases, confused and angered some educators. Typical reactions include "They're not mine!" "No way." "What am I supposed to do?" "Let them come back, but they'll have to do it *my way!*"

As a result of these attitudes and our own turf guarding as special educators, we have sometimes said, "We're giving them back, but we'll still take care of them." A perfect example of this is when we *tutor* our students so that they can pass their regular education classes. Does this not make us expensive tutors? Are we really providing our students special education or is it just slowed-down regular education? Is it our responsibility to provide regular and special education?

Look at the goals you have for yourself as a resource. Are you taking on more than you can realistically be responsible for? Are you making regular education dependent on you? Have you set yourself up to do it all?

Keep in mind that a good resource teacher is often one who gives people helpful information and also assists them in developing the skill to perform a function on their own. This does not make them dependent, but increases their independence and effectiveness.

NOTE: Having completed your questionnaire, you are on your way to becoming an efficient, effective resource in the school. You will find it helpful to review your plan, goals, and objectives on a regular basis and reevaluate both where you are and where you are going. It is a good idea to review your plan every 6 to 8 weeks. You might also find it helpful to carry out your review with one or more of your resourcing colleagues in the district. A group review session can provide you with support and encouragement as well as more ideas for redirection if needed.

KEEPING YOURSELF FIT

Once you are functioning in your role as a resource, there are a number of things you can do to continue supporting yourself. Knowing what you want, what you have to offer, and where you are going is a definite asset. However, this is a *big job*, and it will require a lot of skill, effort, and energy on your part. *Taking care of yourself is essential!*

Here are some further suggestions for keeping yourself *sane*, *happy*, and *secure* in your new job.

Physical Fitness

Get some exercise on a regular basis. Lethargy feeds upon itself and once you have gotten yourself up and out you will feel less stressed, more clear-headed, and more energetic. Find an exercise that fits your style.

Maintain a healthy diet. Skipping meals can put you on an "energy roller-coaster," and you will need your strength. Junk foods do not help. A well-balanced, sensible diet will serve you better.

Meet your requirements for sleep and rest. Whatever amount of sleep you require, try to get that amount.

Psychological Fitness

Promote your own relaxation. Make room for relaxation in your day—every day. Exercise may relax you, or you may do systematic relaxation exercises. Staring off into space for 15 minutes or taking fantasy trips may also do the trick. In any case, remember that relaxation regenerates you.

Keep yourself supported. Establish a network of buddies—a mutual support system. There are times when you need others to lean on, and you can benefit from the resources others have to offer. Cultivate friends who will give you opportunities for laughter, relaxation, support, and enjoyment. Friendly cohorts in special education can be a real asset; those outside your field can expand your horizons.

Follow those hints for psychological health. Learn to say "no" in cases in which you cannot be of help, you know it is not your responsibility, and/or you are not in a position to provide assistance.

Keep things in perspective. Learn to give yourself credit for your successes and recognize places were improvements are needed.

Keep your sense of humor. This is not always easy, but it can make a difference in your stress level and your success in working with others. If you find your environment becoming humorless, try putting humor back in. Establish a "Humor Brigade" in your classroom or building. Given this rather artificial assignment, you will be surprised at how clever your "brigade" can become in finding ways to make people smile and laugh.

Keep a positive outlook. Change may be slow, but keep your plan in mind and proceed systematically.

Work on your time-management strategies. Try to organize your day to maximize your effectiveness. If you find yourself running everywhere—and not as part of your exercise regimen—rearrange your plan and your schedule. Have an organizational master plan that serves your needs.

Release tension in the classroom. If your own classes are wearing you down, plan activities to release the tension. Do systematic relaxation exercises with your class. Make your students more responsible for their own behavior. Remember your sense of humor and theirs!

Mental Fitness

Keep up professionally. Attend workshops, inservice sessions, and staff development activities to stimulate your professional growth. Subscribe to professional journals and participate in professional organizations. These activities can help you avoid getting into a rut, keep you abreast of the latest in your field, and expand your networking possibilities. Also share your good ideas with other professionals: What you may think of as insignificant can be a lifesaver to another teacher.

"Beef up" your weak areas. Recognize areas in which you have limited knowledge and skills and make efforts to remediate these deficits. Visit with cohorts who can assist you. Sign up for relevant courses. *Read!* Try to get your administrator or special education director to offer workshops in your need area.

Develop your talents. Expand your creativity by pursuing your talents. Make sure you make time during the week to pursue activities that are not work related. Incorporate them into your work, if possible. Organize after-school activities for teachers that relate to your talents and talents that others share.

Doing Special Things for Yourself

Splurge. Keep a loose change bank and from time to time spend the money on something special for yourself. Purchase something that gives you pleasure but is not necessarily functional.

Give yourself some special time. Set aside a time period and do something different, fun, or exciting. It might be as simple as an afternoon in the park or as extravagant as a summer cruise. "Getting away from it all" can be rejuvenating—even if it is only for a few minutes.

Give yourself a break. If a situation becomes too frustrating or negative, "let it go" for a brief time. Do not push your plan if it gets too frustrating. Back up, take a break, rethink your goals. Change the plan for a few days—do something different. And do not let the temporary roadblocks cause you to give up. Call your support group or go to dinner. Remember your successes!

2

Being a Resource to Others

Having clarified your goals and objectives as a resource, you are now ready to begin planning your strategy. Keeping in mind your objectives, time constraints, and school climate, you will decide what is most important in terms of your activities, where to begin, and when to start. This chapter provides suggestions regarding strategies. An effort has been made to address categories of activities that often could be included in the role of being a resource. You, of course, have ideas of your own. These suggestions are merely ways to help you start your own planning.

Following is a list of possible job descriptors for your resourcing role:

Salesperson/public relations person.
Communicator/collaborator.
Team member.
Liaison.
Disseminator.

Each of these functions will be discussed separately on the following pages. Your total job description as a resource may include any or all of them. Take what you can and adapt it to your own needs and priorities. Remember your effectiveness as a resource depends, at least in part, on your being confident and comfortable with the role. Make it fit you and your school.

SALESPERSON/PUBLIC RELATIONS PERSON

To be successful as a resource in your school, you must first "sell" your program. Both you and your program must be accepted and respected as worthwhile, necessary parts of the overall school program. Your public relations can have a significant impact on your acceptance and effectiveness. Consequently, the role of "selling" your job should be a high priority and an ongoing activity.

Perhaps you are ambivalent about this role or do not see a great need for it. Take a moment and consider the following often-heard remarks:

"She's got it made—only 8 kids at a time!"

"What an easy job!"

"Oh, you don't know what it's like, teaching 30 kids!" "Those special ed teachers get all the breaks—planning periods, money to buy materials, time to attend workshops, etc., etc."

"What do you mean, he doesn't qualify for special education—What am I supposed to do with him?"

"That's the room where they play games and the kids don't have to do much."

Sound familiar? These complaints hurt special educators and make us angry. They cause barriers between special and regular education and make it difficult to work together as a team. Special educators resent these attitudes, but have we done anything to change them? Have we not inadvertently fostered such complaints if we have not done our "PR"?

How can you overcome this attitude that teachers in special education don't contribute their fair share and have it "so easy"?

Sell Yourself and Sell Your Program!

On Being a Salesperson

1. *Make sure school personnel know who you are and what you do.*

   Think of it as a public relations campaign! Set up some times, places, and situations in which you can do this (e.g., faculty meetings, departmental meetings, PTA meetings, or at lunch). Make sure your audience understands who you are and what you do. Also make sure you let them know what the benefits of your program are to them, the students, and the school.

   Describe who you are:

   "I am a resource teacher. I teach students . . . (giving the who's, what's, and when's), but I also can be a resource to you and help you with students who are in special education programs as well as those who are not . . . . "(Then tell *how* you can be a resource.)

   "I have a resource room. My resource room serves students in the following ways . . . My resource room can also serve you in the following ways . . . " *Be specific* and say only what you can and are willing to provide.

   Present an attitude of: "I am a resource to you and to the students. How can I work with you and be of help to you? How can I make things easier for you as you work with my students and others with special needs?" Do not set yourself up as a savior, martyr, do-it-all, or know-it-all, but rather as a *resource*, a cooperative peer, a member of the school team . . . someone who has important, helpful things to share.

2. *Get out among them.*

Don't just let them *hear* you, let them see you *at work* with your students, being a resource, collaborating with other teachers. *What* they see you doing will have as much, if not more, impact on them than anything else you do! Start talking to people about your work, their needs, or your students. Give them strokes for the legitimately fine work they do. *Ask* whether you can work with them in any way that would be helpful to them!

NOTE: I have emphasized working *with* teachers. Always be careful that you are not telling them what they should do or that you will do it all! Invite teachers to observe in your class—*always* a good selling point when they see how hard you and your students are working and what it is that you do. Ask whether you can teach a class period for them—perhaps do a special session on notetaking, study skills, or test taking. Ask them whether it would be helpful for you to work with a small group in their class on a regular basis rather than taking them out to your room. Suggest that you team teach a lesson with them.

3. *Do ongoing public relations.*

- Have teacher appreciation days. (Let your kids serve punch and cookies and show off their work.)

- Put posters and flyers around the school with helpful suggestions.

- Print a quarterly newsletter with helpful information to regular educators.

- Advertise your services.

- Help organize a teacher support group, if you do not already have one.

- Get free brochures on disabilities and distribute them.

- Help get speakers in for faculty meetings or inservice days.

4. *Watch yourself!*

- If you spend time in the lounge, make sure you are working on something work-related. Be busy!

- Make positive statements about your students. Let teachers know about their progress.

- Do not slip up and make disparaging remarks about any of your professional cohorts. If you have a problem with a peer, try to settle it between the two of you or ask a trusted cohort to help you problem solve in a positive, professional manner.

- Try not to get involved in negative conversations about certain students. Make this an opportunity to offer any services you have that might help these students. Empathize, but do not further this kind of negative discussion by joining in. The teacher may just need to vent frustration. You should not offer more ammunition. Also be sure to protect confidential information.

- Try to win over respected, influential faculty members who can expand your PR efforts. If they see you as a valuable resource, it will influence other faculty members.

- Participate in school-wide functions. Make yourself available and helpful!

5. *Map out a plan.*

- Decide who will be your contacts each week.

- Decide what these contact will consist of (e.g., a speech, written correspondence, in-classroom assistance, a special event, or an awareness session).

- Do not rely on opportunities to arise for doing PR. Your efforts must be *proactive*, coordinated, and effective. Leaving this up to chance will minimize your impact.

Example of an August Activity

- During the summer months, contact banks, insurance companies, and businesses, and ask for donations of freebies to give your faculty members. Often these persons have pens, pencils, rulers, or notepads that they give out for advertising purposes. Get a wide variety of items and place them in bags to give teachers in August. Also include in the bag a description of services, materials, and information you have available to them and services you provide to your students.

- Make an appointment with your building administrator to map out your plans and activities. This person's backing will be crucial to your success. You will most likely receive this support if you have a written plan for review and if you communicate clearcut benefits of your efforts for the staff and your students. Talk about both your long- and short-range plan and why you have set these particular goals. When you get the administrator's approval of your plan, schedule a specific time on the calendar for you to talk with the faculty—the sooner the better! This initial presentation is best done during planning days prior to the opening of school. The topic is "I Am a Resource Teacher—I Have a Resource Room." As the year progresses, you will have other topics of benefit to the staff.

- During this month, try to contact all teachers who have your students. Give them information about the students, when they see you, what they are doing, and forms for teachers to use when contacting you to ask for assistance.

  NOTE: You may have a theory that "If teachers know one of their students is in a special education class, they will prejudge them or expect less of them." This will not happen if you do your groundwork, let the teachers know the facts about the students, make it clear that expectations should not be lowered but that adaptations might be needed and you can work with them to do this.

- Put a flyer out regarding the information and services you have available.

- Make inroads with respected and influential faculty members regarding your resourcing role. Pick two or three and schedule a time to talk with them. Bring something to give them that will benefit them in working with students who have special needs.

COMMUNICATOR/COLLABORATOR

In your role as communicator and collaborator, you will be working with other staff members in your school, particularly those who have your students in their general education classes. Your goal will be to work with teachers to help students succeed in the mainstream. By working together, you and other staff members can develop strategies to assist any student having learning or behavioral difficulties. Such collaboration can have an added benefit of reducing inappropriate referrals to special education.

Unfortunately, collaboration is not always easy to establish between special and general education. However, there is excellent information available that will assist you in this endeavor. Professional journals and other published materials have been focusing on the issue of the special–general education interface for several years. Jeanne Bauwens, Marilyn Friend, Lorna Idol, Marlene Pugach, and Frederick West all have numerous publications on this topic. From their work and that of others, you can obtain many practical suggestions for your collaboration role. (See Appendix.)

Results of research studies regarding collaboration suggest that a first step is to establish a strong supportive base for this role from the school principal. A carefully planned, clear presentation to your principal of what this role will entail, the benefits of this service, and implementation steps will be important in obtaining the support you need. You want the principal to offer his or her backing for the program and communicate this enthusiastically to the staff. Their response to the service may be more positive given this administrative support and leadership.

Once the principal's approval has been obtained, there are a number of steps you may take to implement the service effectively. Your own particular situation will define what the steps will be. However, there are some points for you to keep in mind regarding this role.

The Role of Collaborator

Although I have used the term *collaborator*, collaboration is essentially a *style* of interaction that can enhance problem-solving and planning activities between you and one or more others. This style of communication occurs when parties are viewed as co-equals and they voluntarily agree to work together to address a shared need.

Collaboration is not the same as consultation. Consultation is a process in which an *expert* comes in to help solve a problem. The responsibility is on the consultant to find the answer and make things right. The relationship between the consultant and consultee is not an equal one.

Often resource teachers are placed in the role of consultant. This is a difficult role and one that may create resistance on the part of regular educators. Teachers may resent having a so-called expert come into their class and tell them what they need to do—especially when this person is their co-worker and peer. Consultation can also create situations in which you, the resource teacher, become the person responsible for making the strategy work and the teacher has no ownership in the solution.

As a collaborator, your role shifts from the expert model and you work jointly with teachers. Therefore, you will want to pull back from your "teacher-directing" mode and exhibit a more interactive and sharing style. Your goal is to develop a working, trusting relationship with the teacher that emphasizes shared responsibility and decision making. The two of you will work together to define the problem and develop plans of action. You should be perceived as part of a team approach to problem solving and not as an expert who gives the answers.

Your communication skills will help you reach this goal. Trust, an integral part of a collaborative relationship, is more likely to occur when communication is nonthreatening, nonevaluative and respectful. The teacher should feel "heard" and valued as an integral part of the decision-making process. Both you and the teacher can learn from one another in a give-and-take situation that is future oriented and directed toward solutions.

This collaborative relationship will not always occur immediately and with everyone on staff. Realistically, 100% collaboration may never occur in a school building. You have to be prepared for some resistance and you need to lay the groundwork to increase your chances of success.

Some suggestions for various ways to foster success in your collaboration follow:

- *Develop a collaboration planning team that consists of members from both regular and special education.* This team can explore such issues as benefits of collaboration, incentives, school-wide beliefs about mainstreaming that need to be addressed, and implementation steps. You want the regular education staff to also have ownership in this program and support this process. Having a team set the program, as opposed to just yourself, may make a big difference in its acceptance.

- *Advertise successes.* Have teachers spread the word about the successes of the program. Let the school know how collaboration is working and what benefits have actually occurred.

- *Develop intervention resources.* Your role can be enhanced by developing intervention resources that are accessible to teachers. As ideas are developed among team members, add them to a file. Network with teachers and colleagues in other schools to obtain more ideas. Place these ideas into a workable resource system that teachers can tap into when you are not available.

- *Schedule yourself regularly for collaboration time.* You must be accessible if this service is to work. Your principal is a key player in establishing this time, of course. Establish a system for meeting with teachers that includes the use of "communication forms" to let you know when they are needy and interested.

- *Keep your communication and collaboration skills fine tuned.* Attend staff development activities related to this subject. Be aware that many relevant workshops on this topic are available through business and community organizations as well as educational organizations. Role playing with your special education colleagues can be helpful, as well as brainstorming sessions to develop more intervention strategies. Also, browse through the bookstore to find books on these skills, especially in the business/management section.

These are a few of the many suggestions available to you regarding the communicator/collaborator role. The bottom line is that you need to be seen as an integral part of the school team, working together for student success.

TEAM MEMBER

Akin to the role of collaborator is that of team member. As a team member, you will use your communication and collaboration skills. However, this role is discussed separately to address the part you play as a team member in the building as a whole and as a member of the Admission, Review, and Dismissal Committee.

With the move toward site-based management in schools across the nation, there is a renewed focus on having the campus staff work as a team under the leadership of the principal. What were formerly centralized decision-making responsibilities are now delegated to the campus. Shared decision making and planning among the staff are encouraged. Where do you fit in this scheme? As a special educator, you have an important role on the team, and this is an opportunity for you to have an even greater impact in the school. Your specialized knowledge will be a particular asset in the following areas:

- Collaboration skills.
- Adaptations for students having difficulties in the regular classroom.
- Curriculum modifications.
- Understanding students with special needs.
- Budgeting suggestions for meeting the needs of students with disabilities.
- Developing instructional plans.
- Staff development.

Look back to the questionnaire you completed in Chapter 1 and reconsider the strengths you listed in question 4. Put these in the perspective of your role as a team member. You will quickly realize how these skills can be of benefit to your team. Also, consider your assets in working with your administrator. If you have an administrator who does not have a background in working with special education, you can provide him or her with information regarding the program and students. Find a way to share your expertise in a manner that is non-threatening and facilitative. One way to do this might be to develop a mini-handbook for teachers and ask the principal to review it for accuracy and completeness. If the principal also could benefit from this knowledge, you have given it to him or her in a way that is positive and "face-saving."

As a team member on the Admission, Review, and Dismissal Committee, your role is also vital. Again, your collaboration skills will be valuable in fostering communication and resolving conflicts. As the expert in special education on the team, you may find yourself in a powerful position. Try to counteract attempts to make you the sole controller or dominator of the meeting. Rather, make your role that of rapport builder, facilitator and/or "processor." Following this discussion, an affective checklist is provided that can be used to assist you in this endeavor. To further the positive climate of the meeting, the following suggestions are provided:

- Give parents an advanced organizer prior to the meeting, such as a blank IEP form, an agenda, a progress report on the student, or a checklist of skill areas to be addressed.

- Also give the regular education teacher an advanced organizer.

- As you provide your input in the meeting, have others in the group share their understanding of what you have said and/or respond to your suggestions.

- Be objective in your remarks.

- Listen to both the content and the tone (feeling) of comments.

- Address the problem, not the person. Focus on interests, not positions. (An excellent book on this topic is *Getting to Yes* by Roger Fisher and William Ury, a Penguin book, available in most bookstores in the business/management section.)

- Brainstorm solutions. Be creative. Find common ground.

- Try to find at least one area in which everyone can agree. Do not end a meeting without at least one such agreement—even if the agreement is to meet again!

- Keep the discussion focused on the student, and always find some positives to share.

- Debrief after your meetings from time to time for the purpose of rating how you are functioning as a team. A good idea is to train staff on group processes and team building in an effort to make your meetings as positive and productive as possible. For those of you who have been involved in due process hearings and/or court cases, you will recognize the importance of this recommendation. If you do not have expertise in this area, make sure you find training and resources for yourself. These meetings are an important part of your job, and you are a key member of the team.

AFFECTIVE CHECKLIST FOR ADMISSION, REVIEW, AND DISMISSAL MEETINGS

Satisfactory

Yes ____ No ____ 1. Established a positive beginning (welcome, introductions, process described, everyone comfortable).

Yes ____ No ____ 2. Participants exhibited interest in the proceedings.

Yes ____ No ____ 3. Participants spoke clearly and audibly and were easily understood (professional jargon was avoided).

Yes ____ No ____ 4. All views were respected and considered.

Yes ____ No ____ 5. The child's best interest was the focus.

Yes ____ No ____ 6. No one person dominated the meeting; there was a balance of listening and talking on everyone's part.

Yes ____ No ____ 7. Parent input and understanding were elicited.

Yes ____ No ____ 8. The process encouraged shared decisionmaking.

Yes ____ No ____ 9. Contributions were positive.

Yes ____ No ____ 10. Side conversations were avoided.

Yes ____ No ____ 11. Participants were attentive and displayed good listening skills.

Yes ____ No ____ 12. Questioning strategies encouraged discussion and creative problem-solving, as opposed to "yes," "no," "I don't know" responses.

Yes ____ No ____ 13. Participants reported with confidence and assurance. Everyone was well prepared.

Yes ____ No ____ 14. Participants stayed on task.

Yes ____ No ____ 15. Parents were not overpowered or overwhelmed by staff.

Yes ____ No ____ 16. Conflict was reduced through brainstorming and mediation skills.

Yes ____ No ____ 17. Recommendations included everyone's input (parent input was valued).

Yes ____ No ____ 18. No important issues were dismissed or avoided (even if some decisions/discussions were tabled for a future meeting).

Yes ____ No ____ 19. The meeting ended on a positive note.

Adapted from the affective Checklist for Interdisciplinary Staffings developed by the Department of Special Education, University of Northern Iowa, *Counterpoint* (May/June 1983).

Note: From *Resourcing: Handbook for Special Education Resource Teachers* by Mary Yeomans Jackson, 1992, Reston, VA: The Council for Exceptional Children. Reprinted by permission.

LIAISON

Stepping into the role of liaison may be new for you. However, you probably are already being asked to provide this service to some degree. By *liaison*, I mean acting in the role of intermediary between some agency or organization and your school, special education program, and/or students. This role can be carried out in a number of ways, depending on the specific service to be provided and/or the group or organization with whom you are working. What kind of liaison services you provide will also be based on your school's policy regarding contacts with outside services. Before you consider this role, you must consult with your principal and/or supervisor regarding how you might be a resource in this area. It is important for this person to know what things you are doing as you start and continue in this role.

A good example of how you might be a liaison is working with Juvenile Probation with regard to a student of yours who is involved with this agency. You can be a contact in the school for the probation officer who will check on the student's progress and attendance in school. You can also advise the probation officer of any meetings with the student in which the officer's attendance would be helpful.

Acting as a liaison to camps, clubs, and organizations could also be beneficial. Often parents and students are unaware of free or low-cost activities for students with disabilities. You might develop or obtain copies of listings of such camps, activities, and clubs and share it with parents.

Remember also that many organizations and agencies can be a resource to you. A representative from an organization such as Big Brothers or Big Sisters might be an excellent speaker at a faculty meeting. Many organizations also have useful printed information that can be shared with staff and parents. Since many clubs have community service projects, you might be a contact for them in terms of identifying worthwhile projects. When I was teaching I made friends with an organization that supplied me with "freebies" for rewards for my students and also took my students on several field trips. In turn, I was a speaker at one of their meetings, where I discussed learning disabilities. This, of course, had my principal's blessing, and my students were thrilled. This organization later became active in many school-wide functions that furthered my school PR activities.

My reason for including this section on being a liaison is primarily to remind you of services available outside of your school building. These resources can be valuable to you in your work, and you can also be an important resource to them.

DISSEMINATOR

One of the most rewarding roles you can choose is that of disseminator. Teachers are typically collectors of ideas, articles, and materials—anything that will help them in their teaching. They are especially appreciative of any new ideas that might work in their classroom for the group as a whole or for individual students. You are in a perfect position to assist them. Special education teachers, if anything, are bigger "packrats" than regular education teachers! You often have a wealth of information in the form of both written materials and ideas. Share them!

Sharing Ideas

One good way to disseminate information is simply to share ideas. The information you disseminate does not necessarily have to be written. At times, brief verbal suggestions are effective. One method of sharing your ideas would be to ask your principal for a 5-minute spot on faculty meeting days. At each meeting you could give one effective method for assisting mainstreamed students. For example, you might show teachers how to effectively use advance organizers in presenting information. Other ideas might relate to an effective behavior management tool, test-taking strategies, developing tests or study sheets, and so forth.

Although you might choose to do a longer workshop, sometimes teachers are more responsive and attentive to shorter sessions. Teachers are tired at the end of the school day, and a session longer than 5 or 10 minutes may be too much. As a disseminator of ideas, you want to make sure your audience is responsive!

The cafeteria or lounge may be an ideal setting for communicating ideas to teachers. Many teachers' conversations relate to problem students in their classrooms. Once they have had time to vent—if this seems appropriate—you can collaborate with them on possible ideas for meeting students' needs. By doing this, you can assist teachers in constructive problem solving, as opposed to fostering their "I'm frustrated with this student" talk.

An effective workshop might be to meet with grade-level teachers during their planning period and have them discuss one or two of their most problematic students. You and the teachers could brainstorm possible strategies to work with the student. Again, your job would be to make this a joint problem-solving item and not just a session for venting frustration.

There are, of course, many other methods of sharing ideas and places to do so. Take advantage of situations as they arise! A word of caution, however: Do not become so available that people are *constantly* requesting information from you. If you are busy, set up a specific time and place to discuss their needs—one that is mutually convenient.

Sharing Materials

Disseminating written materials is probably something you are already doing in your job. Special education teachers often receive requests for both student materials and information related to teaching mainstream students. There may be ways in which your materials dissemination can become more organized and more frequent. Various resources are described in Chapter 3. These may help you in expanding your library of available materials.

Some suggestions regarding materials to disseminate include the following:

- Books, workbooks, and worksheets for mainstreamed students.
- Journal articles related to teaching ideas.
- Copies of suggestions for teachers.
- Sample charts or contracts for behavior management plans.
- Sample organizers for students.
- Flyers or brochures related to disabilities and/or services for people with disabilities.
- Workshop flyers.
- Lists that would be helpful to teachers, such as "Survival Words," "Prepositions," and "Commonly Misspelled Words."

Many of the things you share will be based on your particular situation. However, you may want to set up a lending library of helpful materials and regularly disseminate information to the staff. You might choose to have your own weekly flyer or newsletter. You might also disseminate helpful materials at faculty meetings. One excellent idea is to become the clearinghouse for promising practices, new ideas, and teacher-made materials in your school.

A parent volunteer might also assist you in developing a parent-resource library. Parents are often looking for strategies to reinforce academic skills, behavior management ideas, and information on their child's disability and parent organizations. They also need information regarding community services. Any information you could share regarding camps and summer activities would be an excellent resource. Catalogs containing computer programs to reinforce academic skills might also be included. Parents could contribute some of their own resources as well.

Dissemination in General

You, of course, have many ideas related to dissemination of information. You share information all the time—especially information related to your students. This information is very important in terms of the students' succeeding in the mainstream. Teachers need to know what they can expect from the student and how to meet the student's needs. Begin sharing information as soon as possible and *before* a particular child is placed, if feasible.

Enjoy the role of disseminator. Teachers will appreciate your efforts, and as a result, so will your students. Do not forget your special education cohorts throughout the school system. They can be resources as well as users of your system.

TIME MANAGER

In the preceding pages, several possible roles have been described for you as a resource to others. An obvious big question remains: *Where do you find the time to do these things?*

There are no simple solutions to this problem, but some suggestions are listed below.

1. *Analyze how you are currently using your time.* Take a few days to keep a log of how your time is spent. A sample log is included on the following page. After completing your log, look for time periods that could be better used to implement your resourcing role. A worksheet for this analysis is also provided.

2. *Look at specific activities you are currently doing and brainstorm ways to complete them more efficiently and effectively.* For example, if you have an aide, could some of your duties be delegated to this person? Are there legitimate opportunities for you and another teacher to combine classes in order for each of you to be free for other important job responsibilities? Perhaps you could trade off with each other. Is your work organized in such a way that you tackle the difficult, important items first and then move on to less demanding activities? Or do you find yourself putting off your least favorite activities and spending time on nonessentials? Critically examine your own organization and rearrange some activities that could be completed more efficiently. I recommend that you tackle first the most important tasks or those that are most difficult and time consuming.

3. *Talk with your principal about options in scheduling.* If your schedule provides no time for some of the roles mentioned earlier, talk with your principal about possible schedule changes. When you do this, be prepared to discuss the importance of these roles, the goals and benefits of your resourcing role, and suggested options. One benefit of collaboration is that referrals to special education are often reduced through preventative strategies. This could reduce the amount of time you are required to test.

4. *If you have a collaboration planning team, have them brainstorm ways to schedule time for this activity.* Some schools have agreed to have roving substitutes once a week for this purpose. Others have reduced staff meeting time to allow for collaboration.

5. *Remember your goals and priorities.* Do not overdo it as you start in your resourcing role. Do not tackle more than you can handle!

6. *Keep an ongoing watch on your time.* Once you have begun your time-management strategies, keep using them!

TIME LOG

Time	Direct Instruction	Lesson Planning	Testing	Observations	Paperwork	Meetings	Required School Duties/Homework	Conferences	Breaks/Lunch/Other
7:30 - 7:45									
7:45 - 8:00									
8:00 - 8:15									
8:15 - 8:30									
8:30 - 8:45									
8:45 - 9:00									
9:00 - 9:15									
9:15 - 9:30									
9:30 - 9:45									
9:45 - 10:00									
10:00 - 10:15									
10:15 - 10:30									
10:30 - 10:45									
10:45 - 11:00									
11:00 - 11:15									
11:15 - 11:30									
11:30 - 11:45									
11:45 - 12:00									
12:00 - 12:15									
12:15 - 12:30									
12:30 - 12:45									
12:45 - 1:00									
1:00 - 1:15									
1:15 - 1:30									
1:30 - 1:45									
1:45 - 2:00									
2:00 - 2:15									
2:15 - 2:30									
2:30 - 2:45									
2:45 - 3:00									
3:00 - 3:15									
3:15 - 3:30									
3:30 - 3:45									
3:45 - 4:00									

Note: From Bauwens, J., & Ehlert, B. (1983). Collaborative endeavors. Nonprofit educational newsletter. Boise, ID. (Copyright 1983). Adapted by permission.
Note: From Resourcing: Handbook for Special Education Resource Teachers by Mary Yeomans Jackson, 1992, Reston, VA: The Council for Exceptional Children. Reprinted by permission.

ANALYSIS-OF-TIME LOG

Comments about your use of time today:

Was your day organized to maximize your goals?　　Yes ＿＿　　No ＿＿

If no, what time periods, if any, were wasted?

What interruptions occurred, if any? How many?

What did you dislike about how you used your time?

How could you have improved your use of time?

Note: From *Resourcing: Handbook for Special Education Resource Teachers* by Mary Yeomans Jackson, 1992, Reston, VA: The Council for Exceptional Children. Reprinted by permission.

3

Accessing Resources

A major part of your resourcing job is to provide information, support, and resources to students, teachers, parents, agency personnel, and others. In order to be effective in this role, you must be a master at accessing resources. In many school districts, there is not a plethora of materials available to resource teachers for this purpose. Some districts have a centralized special education resource library, but this is not always convenient to teachers. Moreover, your *resource room* will be considered by many to be the place to go to find support, information, and materials. By organizing a mini-resource library within your classroom, you will be providing a valuable service to the school and fulfilling an essential resourcing role.

The following pages provide information regarding places and people who can provide resources to you at little or no cost. The types and kinds of resources you access will depend on your own situation. However, over time, you can accumulate a variety of materials that will be of assistance to your clientele. It is helpful to remember that you operate as a sort of reference librarian to many people in your job. Your effectiveness is, in part, directly related to the number of effective resources you can provide to others.

HUMAN RESOURCES

You already have available to you many people who can be resources, providing both materials and support. Other resource teachers in your district can offer valuable assistance to your program. Many of them will have materials that you can duplicate for your mini-library. These may include teaching materials as well as parent materials, informative brochures and flyers, resource listings, and catalogs. If resource teachers in your district meet regularly, suggest that one of your meetings be a sharing session in which teachers exchange both ideas and resource materials. Another idea would be to rotate meetings around the district and tour each other's rooms and resources. Your cohorts can also provide you with support, training, and ideas for effective resourcing. As a group, you may want to jointly develop needed resource materials that everyone can use. You might also set up a speaker's bureau in order to access the expertise of others in your district.

Do not overlook the resources available through your regular education staff. Teachers often have much valuable information on effective teaching strategies, homework ideas, and community resources. A file system of effective techniques for addressing specific academic or behavioral problems could be particularly helpful to the staff as a whole. Volunteer to organize and house such a resource system. Regular education teachers work with mainstreamed students daily. Tap into their expertise on effective ways to deal with these students. Get their ideas down on paper and share them.

Your students can also assist you in this endeavor. Since many of them need to develop organizational skills, teach them the organization of your own library. Have them file and shelve materials. Teach them how to check materials in and out. When new materials are added, let them categorize and enter these additions into the system.

Remember also that your students can be an excellent resource within your program as study buddies, peer tutors, and aides. Cooperative learning strategies can be effective. Let students learn from each other as well as from you.

Other human resources include parents, agency personnel, and others in the community. A parent volunteer could be quite helpful in setting up your library and maintaining it. Often parents have helpful resources that they are willing to share with others. If you have actively involved parents, suggest that they set up a parent resource library in your room. They may be able to provide support and suggestions to other parents of students with disabilities.

Contact agency and community resources for useful free materials. These may include references, directories, and program information. Some community organizations may be willing to donate items for your reinforcement program or funds to obtain helpful resources. Consult with your principal regarding the feasibility of contacting such groups.

There are probably other human resources available within your community. Of course, all this takes time, but it is time well spent. The information you provide may be crucial in helping a student succeed in the mainstream. It may give parents exactly what they need to help the family function effectively.

TOLL-FREE TELEPHONE SERVICES

Some excellent free or low-cost resources are available outside your community. Many of these contacts have printed information that can be obtained easily. Access ERIC; 1-800-USE-ERIC is an invaluable resources. The service was created to provide accessibility to the Educational Resources Information Center (ERIC), perhaps the largest source of education information in the United States. Staff at this number can provide answers to your questions, make referrals, and send ERIC publications. The ERIC Clearinghouse on Handicapped and Gifted Children, located at The Council for Exceptional Children, is part of this system. Their direct line is 703/264-9474. Many useful and informative materials are available through this service.

Other helpful toll-free telephone services include the following:

American Association on Mental Retardation	1-800-424-3688
American Council of the Blind	1-800-424-8666
American Diabetes Association	1-800-232-3472
American Foundation for the Blind	1-800-232-5463
American Paralysis Association	1-800-225-1292
Association for Retarded Citizens of the U.S.	1-800-433-5255
Better Hearing Institute Helpline	1-800-424-8576
Captioned Films for the Deaf	1-800-237-6213
Center for Special Education Technology Information Exchange	1-800-345-8324
Division of Rehabilitation Services	1-800-537-2549
Epilepsy Foundation of America	1-800-332-1000
ERIC Clearinghouse on Adult Cases and Continuing Education	1-800-848-4815
HEATH (Higher Education and the Handicapped Resource Center)	1-800-54-HEATH
Job Accommodation Network	1-800-526-7234
Job Opportunities for the Blind	1-800-638-7518
National Alliance of Blind Students	1-800-424-8666
National Association for Hearing and Speech Action (V/TDD)	1-800-638-8255
National Association for Parents of the Visually Impaired	1-800-562-6265
National Child Abuse Hotline	1-800-4-A-CHILD
National Committee for Citizens in Education	1-800-NETWORK

Note: From *Resourcing: Handbook for Special Education Resource Teachers* by Mary Yeomans Jackson, 1992, Reston, VA: The Council for Exceptional Children. Reprinted by permission.

National Down Syndrome Congress	1-800-232-6372
National Down Syndrome Society	1-800-221-4602
National Easter Seal Society	1-800-221-6827
National Head Injury Foundation	1-800-444-NHIF
National Health Information Clearinghouse	1-800-336-4797
National Information Center on Deaf-Blindness	1-800-672-6720
National Information Systems for Health Related Services	1-800-922-9234
National Organization on Disability	1-800-248-ABLE
National Rehabilitation Information Center (V/TDD)	1-800-34-NARIC
National Speech Needs Center (TDD)	1-800-833-3232
Orton Dyslexia Society	1-800-233-1222
Resource Center for the Handicapped	1-800-22-SHARE
Retinitis Pigmentosa Foundation Fighting Blindness	1-800-638-2300
Social Security Administration	1-800-234-5772

If you are fortunate to work in a district that is a member of SpecialNET, you have a wealth of information accessible to you. Find out from your administration whether your district subscribes and whether you can use this computer service. The number for information regarding SpecialNET is 1-800-634-5644.

PARENT RESOURCES

There are numerous resources available to parents of students with disabilities. Some reference are listed here to help you get started in this area. One excellent resource is the Pacer Center, which is an organization for parents of students with disabilities. They have many resources that can be purchased. Their address is 4826 Chicago Avenue South, Minneapolis, MN (1-800-53-PACER).

Other organizations that parents may wish to join have numerous resources you can access. Three of these are:

Learning Disabilities Association
4156 Library Road
Pittsburgh, PA 15234
412/341-1515

Federation of Families for Children's Mental Health
1021 Prince Street
Alexandria, VA 22314-2971
703/684-7710

Note: From *Resourcing: Handbook for Special Education Resource Teachers* by Mary Yeomans Jackson, 1992, Reston, VA: The Council for Exceptional Children. Reprinted by permission.

Orton Dyslexia Society
724 York Road
Baltimore, MD 21204
1-800-222-3123

Other sources of information for parents include:

Gladd Kids
(Nonprofit support/information ADHD students)
P.O. Box 62
Nutley, NJ 07110
201/235-0942

Challenge, Inc.
(Newsletter for parents on ADHD)
P.O. Box 2001
West Newburg, MA 01985

Reading Is Fundamental
(Practical tips for parents to encourage reading)
600 Maryland Avenue S.W.
Washington, DC 20024

Helping Your Child Succeed in School
School Division, AAP
220 East 23rd Street
New York, NY 10010

Exceptional Parent
P.O. Box 3000
Department EP
Denville, NJ 07834

National Center for Learning Disabilities
99 Park Avenue
New York, NY 10016

National Information Center for Handicapped Children and Youth
P.O. Box 1492
Washington, DC 20013

Committee for Children
(Nonprofit organization for the prevention of child abuse)
172 20th Avenue
Seattle, WA 98122
206/322-5050

Note: From *Resourcing: Handbook for Special Education Resource Teachers* by Mary Yeomans Jackson, 1992, Reston, VA: The Council for Exceptional Children. Reprinted by permission.

INSTRUCTIONAL RESOURCES

Information to assist you in providing teaching suggestions to staff members and others is available from a variety of resources. Many resources are free or low cost. Some of these may also assist you in your own teaching or in providing program support strategies for parents.

For a wealth of sources, consider purchasing *The Educators Desk Reference: A Sourcebook of Educational Information and Research*, MacMillan Publishing Co., 866 Third Avenue, New York, NY 10022 ($49.95). This is a catalog of major information resources.

There are several sourcebooks of free or low cost teaching aids. One that is revised annually is *Educators Grade Guide to Free Teaching Aids*, Educators Progress Service, Inc., Randolph, WI 53956. This company publishes a number of other guides on subjects such as free computer materials, guidance materials, and so forth. Each sourcebook costs approximately $20.00 to $45.00.

Other sources to guide you to instructional resources include:

U.S. Department of Education
Office of Special Education and Rehabilitative Services
Office of the Assistant Secretary, Room 3006 MES, Mail Stop 2525
330 C Street S.W.
Washington, DC 20202
202/732-1265

Educators Guide to Effective Special Education Materials
Instructional Materials Center
Division of Special Education
229 State House
Indianapolis, IN 46204
317/232-0579

ERIC Clearinghouse on Handicapped and Gifted Children
The Council for Exceptional Children
1920 Association Drive
Reston, VA 22091-1589
703/620-3660

Master Directory: Research Projects Currently Funded by U.S. Department of Education
Office of Special Education and Rehabilitative Services
Office of Special Programs, Division of Innovation and Development
Washington, DC 20202
(NOTE: This publication gives names and addresses for research projects currently funded by the U.S. Department of Education, Office of Special

Note: From *Resourcing: Handbook for Special Education Resource Teachers* by Mary Yeomans Jackson, 1992, Reston, VA: The Council for Exceptional Children. Reprinted by permission.

Education Programs. Many of these projects have excellent printed resources and information that can be ordered.)

Dropout Prevention: A Book of Sources is an excellent resource published by The National Committee for Citizens in Education (NCCE), 10840 Little Patuxent Parkway, Suite 301, Columbia, MD 21044. A number of information clearinghouses are listed in this book, included NCCE. Their number is 1-800-638-9675. This organization, in addition to having many resources related to school improvement, has a newspaper and toll-free advice line for parents.

The New Reading Teacher's Book of Lists
Prentice-Hall Inc.
Englewood Cliffs, NJ 07632

Tell 'em Ware Tattler
1714 Olson Way
Marshalltown, IA 50158

Professional Journals

Professional journals are an excellent source of information on effective teaching strategies. Following is a list of some that are relevant to resource programs. Although many of these journals are available through membership in organizations such as The Council for Exceptional Children, in some cases single copies may also be ordered for particular articles of interest to you.

Augmentative Communication	1-800-638-6423
Behavioral Disorders	703/620-3660
Better Teaching	703/528-5840
Children's Legal Rights Journal	1-800-828-7571
Education Daily	703/683-4100
Education of the Handicapped	703/683-4100
Education Week	202/364-4114
Education USA	703/528-6560
Educational Leadership	703/549-9110
Exceptional Children	703/620-3660
The Executive Educator	703/838-6749
Federal Assistance Monitor	1-800-666-6380
Infants and Young Children	301/698-7140
Journal of Head Trauma	1-800-638-8437
Journal of Learning Disabilities	512/451-3246

Note: From *Resourcing: Handbook for Special Education Resource Teachers* by Mary Yeomans Jackson, 1992, Reston, VA: The Council for Exceptional Children. Reprinted by permission.

Journal of Special Education Technology	703/620-3600
LD Forum	913/492-8755
Learning Disabilities Focus	703/620-3600
Learning Disabilities Research	703/620-3600
Mental and Physical Disability Law Report	202/331-2240
Phi Delta KAPPAN	1-800-833-NCEC
Remedial and Special Education	512/451-3246
School Law News	1-800-666-7444
Special Education and the Handicapped	1-800-328-5664
TEACHING Exceptional Children	703/620-3660

Publishing Companies

Having catalogs of major publishing companies available is also a good idea. Teachers often are looking for specific materials to order and do not know where to look. Following is a listing of some major publishing companies:

Addison Wesley
2725 Sand Hill Road
Menlo Park, CA 94025
1-800-447-2226

American Guidance Services
Circle Pines, MN 55014
612/786-4343

Aspen Publishers, Inc.
1600 Research Boulevard
Rockville, MD 20850
1-800-638-8437

Attainment Company
P.O. Box 103
Oregon, WI 53575
1-800-327-4269

Beckley-Cardy (Mid-America Region)
1645 Downs Drive
West Chicago, IL 60185
1-800-227-1178

Britannica
425 N. Michigan Avenue
Chicago, IL 60611
1-800-621-3900

Center for Humanities
Communications Park
Box 100
Mount Kisco, NY 10549-0010
1-800-431-1242

Communication School Builders
P.O. Box 42050
Tucson, AZ 85733
602/323-7500

CTB/McGraw-Hill
2500 Garden Road
Monterey CA 93940
1-800-538-9547

Note: From *Resourcing: Handbook for Special Education Resource Teachers* by Mary Yeomans Jackson, 1992, Reston, VA: The Council for Exceptional Children. Reprinted by permission.

Curriculum Associates
5 Esquire Road
N. Billerica, MA 01862
1-800-225-0248

EDMARK
P.O. Box 3903
Bellevue, WA 98009-3903
1-800-426-0856

DLM
One DLM Park
Allen, TX 75002
1-800-527-4747

Educational Center
1410 Mill Street
Greensboro, NC
1-800-334-0298

Educational Activities
P.O. Box 392
Freeport, NY 11520
1-800-645-4666

Educational Teaching Aids
3905 Bohannon Drive
Menco, CA
415/322-9934

Good Apple
1204 Buchanan Street
P.O. Box 299
Carthage, IL 62321-0299
1-800-435-7234

Harcourt Brace Jovanovich, Inc.
Dowden Road
Orlando, FL 32887
1-800-225-5425

Hartley Courseware, Inc.
133 Bridge Street
Box 419
Dimondale, MI 48821
1-800-247-1380

Lakeshore Lifeskills
2695 E. Dominguez
Reston, VA 22091-1589
703/620-3660

Lingui Systems
3100 4th Avenue
P.O. Box 747
East Moline, IL 61233
1-800-ALL-TIME

Love Publishing Company
1777 South Bellaire Street
Denver, CO 80222
303/757-2579

Macmillan/McGraw-Hill
Highstown, NJ 08520
1-800-843-8855

Opportunities for Learning
20417 Nordhoff Street
Dept. 9HA
Chadanth, CA 91311
818/341-2535

Peekan Publications, Inc.
P.O. Box 513
Freeport, IL 61032
1-800-345-7335

Preston Bissell
60 Page Road
Clifton, NJ 07012
1-800-631-7277

Pro-Ed
8700 Shoal Creek Boulevard
Austin, TX 78758
512/451-3246

Project Special Education
Box 31
Sauk Centre, MN 56378-0031
1-800-255-0752

Note: From *Resourcing: Handbook for Special Education Resource Teachers* by Mary Yeomans Jackson, 1992, Reston, VA: The Council for Exceptional Children. Reprinted by permission.

Scholastic
Box 6502
Jefferson, MO 65102
1-800-325-6149

Sunburst
39 Washington Avenue
Pleasantville, NY 10570-2898
1-800-431-1934

Steck Vaughn
P.O. Box 26015
Austin, TX 78755
1-800-531-5015

SVE
1345 Diversey Parkway
Chicago IL 60614
1-800-829-1900

Remember, also, that publishing companies sometimes have free samples of materials and/or policies for previewing materials.

OTHER NATIONAL RESOURCES

Aid to Adoption of Special Kids
3530 Grand Avenue
Oakland, CA 94610
415/451-1748

American Diabetes Association
505 8th Avenue
New York, NY 10018
212/947-9707

American Foundation for the Blind, Inc.
15 West 16th Street
New York, NY 10011
212/620-2000

American Heart Association
7320 Greenville Avenue
Dallas, TX 75231
214/750-5414

American Printing House for the Blind
1839 Frankfort Avenue
P.O. Box 6085
Louisville, KY 40206
502/895-2405

Note: From *Resourcing: Handbook for Special Education Resource Teachers* by Mary Yeomans Jackson, 1992, Reston, VA: The Council for Exceptional Children. Reprinted by permission.

Boy Scouts of America
Scouting for the Handicapped
1325 Walnut Hill Lane
Irving, TX 75038-3096
214/580-2000

Camp Fire Girls, Inc.
4601 Madison Avenue
Kansas City, MO 64112
816/756-1950

Center for Innovation in Teaching the Handicapped
Indiana University
2805 E. 10th Street, Room 150
Bloomington, IN 47415
812/335-5848

The Council for Exceptional Children
CEC Information Services
1920 Association Drive
Reston, VA 22091-1589
703/620-3660

Cystic Fibrosis Foundation
6931 Arlington Road
Bethesda, MD 20814
301/951-4422

Epilepsy Foundation of America
4351 Garden City Drive
Landover, MD 20785
301/459-3700

Gallaudet School for the Deaf
800 Florida Avenue N.E.
Washington, DC 20002
202/651-5000

Girl Scouts of the USA
Scouting for the Handicapped
Girl's Program
830 Third Avenue
New York, NY 10022
212/940-7500

Note: From *Resourcing: Handbook for Special Education Resource Teachers* by Mary Yeomans Jackson, 1992, Reston, VA: The Council for Exceptional Children. Reprinted by permission.

Goodwill Industries of America, Inc.
9200 Wisconsin Avenue
Bethesda, MD 20814
301/530-6500

Guide Dog Foundation for the Blind
371 East Jericho Turnpike
Smithtown, NY 11787
516/944-8900

Helen Keller National Center for Deaf-Blind Youths and Adults
111 Middle Neck Road
Sands Point, NY 11050
516/944-8900

Human Resources Center
I.U. Willets Road
Albertson, NY 11507
516/747-5400

International Reading Association
Box 8139
Newark, DE 19711
302/731-1600

Lions Club International
300 22nd Street
Oak Brook, IL 60570
312/571-5466

Mental Disability Legal Resource Center Commission
    on the Mentally Disabled, American Bar Association
1800 M Street, N.W.
Washington, DC 20036
202/331-2240

Muscular Dystrophy Association, Inc.
810 Seventh Avenue
New York, NY 10019
212/586-0808

National Association of the Deaf
814 Thayer Avenue
Silver Spring, MD 20910
301/587-1788

Note: From *Resourcing: Handbook for Special Education Resource Teachers* by Mary Yeomans Jackson, 1992, Reston, VA: The Council for Exceptional Children. Reprinted by permission.

National Association for Retarded Citizens
P.O. Box 6109
Arlington, TX 76006
817/640-0204

National Easter Seal Society for Crippled Children and Adults
2023 West Ogden Avenue
Chicago, IL 60612
312/243-8400

National Institute of Dyslexia
3200 Woodline Street
Chevy Chase, MD 20815
301/652-0942

National Institute for Rehabilitation Engineering
97 Decker Road
Butler, NJ 07405
201/838-2500

National Organization for Rare Disorders, Inc.
P.O. Box 8923
New Fairfield, CT 06812
203/746-6518

National Society for Autistic Children
1234 Massachusetts, N.W., #1017
Washington, DC 20005
202/783-0125

Spina Bifida Association of America
1700 Rockville Pike, #540
Rockville, MD 20852
301/770-7222

The Association for Persons with Severe Handicaps (TASH)
7010 Roosevelt Way, N.E.
Seattle, WA 98115
206/523-8446

United Cerebral Palsy Associations, Inc.
66 East 34th Street
New York, NY 10016
212/481-6300

Note: From *Resourcing: Handbook for Special Education Resource Teachers* by Mary Yeomans Jackson, 1992, Reston, VA: The Council for Exceptional Children. Reprinted by permission.

FINAL COMMENTS

This chapter has only skimmed the surface of resources available to you. You will want to add your own resources. The following page is a place to include these important names and telephone numbers.

As mentioned earlier, it takes time and effort to access resources. I recommend that you consider this an ongoing, long-term project. Enlist volunteers and/or students to assist you. Do consider it part of your resourcing job, however. It is important, and it will make your job easier in the long run. By having information and resources easily accessible, you will not be "reinventing the wheel" on a regular basis and you will not constantly be engaged in "search missions." Teachers, parents, and others will also be most appreciative of the information you have to share!

SOURCES

Name	Address	Telephone

Conclusion

Your job as a resource within the school is not an easy one. However, it can be a rewarding one. Staff, parents, students, and others see you as a source of help and assistance. You are the relief or recovery to many people in the school.

Hopefully, this book has assisted you in this endeavor. We have come a long way in special education, and it is nice to know that special educators are considered an integral part of the school. Now that we have been launched into the mainstream, we have an opportunity to show how effective our resources are and how we truly model the definition of *resource*.

You *can* do it all and do it well! Just remember, being a resource to others also means you must be a resource to yourself!

Appendix
Communicator/Collaborator References

Bauwens, J., Hourcade, J., & Friend, M. (1989). Cooperative teaching: A model for general and special education integration. *Remedial and Special Education, 10,* 17–22.

Chalfont, J. C., Pysh, M. V., & Moultrice, R. (1979). Teacher assistance teams: A model for within-building problem solving. *Learning Disability Quarterly, 2,* 85–96.

Council of Administrators of Special Education (CASE). (1989). *An effective interface between regular and special education: A synopsis of issues and successful practices.* Information dissemination packet. Indiana University: CASE Research Committee.

Friend, M. (Ed.). (1988). Dimensions of school consultation practice. [Special issue]. *Remedial and Special Education, 9,* 1–62.

Friend, M., & McNutt, G. (1984). Resource room programs: Where are we now? *Exceptional Children, 51,* 150–155.

Idol, L., Paolucci-Whitcomb, P., & Nevin, A. (1986). *Collaborative consultation.* Rockville, MD: Aspen Publishers.

Idol-Maestas, L. (1983). *Special educators consultation handbook.* Austin, TX: Pro-Ed.

Johnson, D., & Johnson, R. (1980). The key to effective inservice: Building teacher-teacher collaboration. *The Developer,* 223–236.

Margolis, H., & McGettigan, J. (1988). Managing resistance to instructional modifications in mainstreamed environments. *Remedial and Special Education, 9,* 15–21.

Minotti, A. T. (1990). *CREATE: Coordinate resources efficiently and team effectively.* Trumbull, CT: Trumbull Public Schools.

Wang, M. C., Reynolds, M. C., & Walberg, H. J. (1986). Rethinking special education. *Educational Leadership, 9,* 26–31.

West, J. Frederick, & Idol, L. (1989). *Collaboration in the schools*. Austin, TX: Pro-Ed.

Two excellent publications:

Remedial and Special Education (RASE). [All issues]. Austin, TX: Pro-Ed.

Journal of Educational and Psychological Consultation. [All issues]. Hillside, NJ: Erlbaum.

Also, Lynne Cook and Marilyn Friend gave an excellent presentation on collaboration at The Council for Exceptional Children's 68th Annual Convention, Toronto, Ontario, April, 1990. Perhaps you can find materials from this session.